Creative Knitting for all Seasons and Yarns

Skill Level: Beginners to Advanced

SUE JOHNSON

Published in Australia by Butterfly Knit Designs
Email: sue@butterflyknitdesigns.com
Website: www.butterflyknitdesigns.com

First published in Australia 2016
Copyright © Susan Johnson 2016

All rights reserved. No part of this publication may be reproduced, stored in a retrieval system, or transmitted, in any form or by any means without the prior written permission of the publisher, nor be otherwise circulated in any form of binding or cover other than that in which it is published and without a similar condition being imposed on the subsequent purchaser.

National Library of Australia Cataloguing-in-Publication entry

Creator: Johnson, Sue, author.

Title: Creative knitting for all seasons and yarns : skill level beginners to advanced / Sue Johnson.

ISBN: 9780987353122 (paperback)

Subjects: Knitwear.
Knitting--Patterns.
Yarn--Coloring.
Color decoration and ornament.

Dewey Number: 746.432041
Original edition - Butterfly Wings ISBN: 978-0-9873531-0-8
978-0-9873531-2-2 (printed book)
978-0-9873531-3-9 (ebook)

Cover photography by Natalie Davies
Cover and formatting by Nelly Murariu
Cover and formatting of the original edition by Jodie Zidar

Printed by Minuteman Press Glen Waverley
Typeset in Helvetica Neue LT Std, 55 Roman, 10pt on 12pt

Disclaimer
All care has been taken in the preparation of the information herein, but no responsibility can be accepted by the publisher or author for any damages resulting from the misinterpretation of this work. All contact details given in this book were current at the time of publication, but are subject to change.

The advice given in this book is based on the experience of the individuals. Professionals should be consulted for individual problems. The author and publisher shall not be responsible for any person with regard to any loss or damage caused directly or indirectly by the information in this book.

CONTENTS

Creative Knitting for all Seasons and Yarns 5

Dual Yarn Summer Top 7

Rainbow Wrap 9

Confetti Top 11

Flounce Scarf (Noro Silk Garden) 13

Flounce Scarf (Wool Blend) 14

Flounce Scarf (Noro Kureyon Sock Yarn) 15

Ribbon Yarn Wrap 17

Bella 19

Multi Yarn Wrap 21

Scarf & Hat in Shades of Autumn 25

Fuzzy Scarf & Hat 27

Sunset Scarf 29

Moth Cocoon 31

Butterfly Cocoon 33

Dragonfly Wrap 35

Bobbly Wrap 37

Pastel Scarf 39

Butterfly Blanket 41

Framed Butterflies 47

Butterfly Cushion 48

Contributors 51

ABOUT SUE JOHNSON

Sue Johnson has been designing hand-knits since her children were young in the 70's. A love of colour motivated Sue to design hand-knits incorporating hand-dyed and hand-spun yarns. Sue has presented creative knitting workshops at the Embroiderers' Guild and Brighton Recreation Centre in Melbourne.

Sue has also developed and given presentations on the Art of Knitting. Sue originally studied and taught mathematics, then changed career to work as a registered nurse. Sue's recent work has been in research at Monash University.

Sue hopes this book will inspire others to explore the possibilities of creating unique knitted items and enjoy the same pleasure she has experienced creating original hand-knits.

For information regarding Creative Knitting Workshops see Sue's website *www.butterflyknitdesigns.com.*

CREATIVE KNITTING FOR ALL SEASONS AND YARNS

Skill Level: Beginners to Advanced

Each of us is a unique individual. Each design presented in this book is unique. My intention in providing details of how each design was produced is not for the design to be replicated exactly, but for the reader to gain insight into the possible processes which can be utilised to produce your own individual creative designs.

The instructions provide guidelines for choosing combinations of colours, textures and plies. There is an endless array of possible combinations of colours and textures waiting to be discovered by you. Enjoy the process of experimentation. Put aside any self-imposed needs for producing the perfect copy.

Don't be afraid to make mistakes; this fear restricts your creativity. Many times I have pulled undone attempts at combinations of yarns and choices of needles when the result has not been as pleasing to the eye as I had hoped. Having discarded a yarn from one design, I often find it perfect in a different combination.

In this collection are designs using a single yarn, and designs using two or more yarns in combination. Each design is a simple shape. Altering the size to your requirements is a simple matter of adding a few more stitches to the number cast on and knitting a few more rows to adjust for width or length. You can substitute any similar weight yarn using the yardage, i.e. length per 50gm ball, as an indicator.

I have included designs using the techniques of short rows, dropped stitches, colour shading and the use of reverse stocking stitch to create a picture. There are endless possibilities of creating your own original designs incorporating these techniques.

My hope is that you experience the enjoyment that I have felt as each unique design is produced, and that you will be proud to display your individuality expressed in your choice of colour and texture. Just as the butterfly is free to fly, your creativity can be set free when you detach from the limitations of what the end result should be, and explore the limitless possibilities of what the end result can be. Set your creativity free to fly.

Yarns Combined to Create Unique Knitted Fabrics

Photo: Flounce Scarf
(Wool Blend - multi colour)

Photo: Dual Yarn Summer Top

BEGINNERS

DUAL YARN SUMMER TOP

Yarn: Summer Top

Materials

4(5) x 50g balls 4ply cotton.

4(5) x 50g balls Polyester ladder yarn.

Needles: 5mm or required size to give correct tension.

Fits: Bust Small 90cm (Medium 100cm).

Measures: 96cm (108cm).

Length: 48cm (55cm).

Tension: 16sts to 10cm with two yarns knitted together.

Instructions

Front

» Cast on 80sts (90sts).

» Work in garter stitch (knit every row) till work measures 48cm (55cm) in length.

Back

» Work as for front.

To make up

» Sew side seams from bottom edge to 20cm (24cm) from top edge.

» Sew 12cm (14cm) shoulder seam.

Diagram

48cm (55cm)

96cm (108cm)

Alternative colours

Photo: Rainbow Wrap

INTERMEDIATE

RAINBOW WRAP

Yarn: Rainbow Wrap

Materials

1 x (2,2) 100g ball Adriafil Baba 100% Merino Wool, Colour 62 (60m per 50g).

1 x (2,2) 50g balls Moda Vera Jessica 80% acrylic, 20% mohair (190m per 50g), Colour black.

Needles: 8mm

Sizes: Small, Medium, Large.

Instructions

» Using Jessica acrylic/mohair, cast on 95sts (103sts, 111sts).

» Knit 2 rows.

» Using the Baba wool, knit one row.

» Using Jessica acrylic/mohair, knit 4 rows.

» Repeat the last 5 rows till work measures approximately 28cm (30cm, 32cm).

» Using Jessica acrylic/mohair, cast off tightly. (Cast off edge is shorter than cast on edge).

» Gather one edge (C-D) using a running thread of yarn to a length of 6cm (7cm, 8cm).

» Sew this gathered side edge (C-D) to the beginning of the cast off row (A-B) as shown in diagram.

Diagram

A   B
                          C
Cast off row 6cm (7cm, 8cm)

Cast on row 124cm (134cm, 148cm)
                          D

Alternative colour

Photo: Confetti Top

INTERMEDIATE

CONFETTI TOP

Yarn: Confetti top

Materials

10 (12) x 50g balls S Charles Collezione Venus Viscose Polyamide Yarn (75m, 50g; 95% viscose, 5% polyamide) Colour; Black Brights Multi 007.

Needles: 5.5mm

Fits: Bust approximately, Small 32in (81-86cm), Medium 34in (86-91cm).

Measures: 88cm (93cm).

Length: approximately 53cm (58cm).

Tension: 12sts to 10cm.

Instructions

Front

- » Using 5.5mm needles and two strands of yarn together cast on 59 (65) stitches.
- » Rows 1-8: Knit 8 rows.
- » Row 9: *Knit 1 winding yarn (2 strands) around needle three times, repeat from *to end.
- » Row 10: Knit to end dropping the extra loops.
- » Repeat these 10 rows 10 (11) times.
- » Knit 7 rows.
- » Cast off.

Back

- » Work as for front.
- » Sew sides together to 35cm (36cm) from bottom edge, leaving 18cm (22cm) armhole opening.
- » Sew shoulders to make 10cm (12cm) shoulder seam.

Alternative Version

Substitute Materials

8 (10) x 50g balls Filatura Di Crosa Brilla (110m, 50g, 42% Cotton, 58% Viscose) Colour 447 Orange.

Alternative colour

Photo: Flounce Scarf (Noro Silk Garden)

INTERMEDIATE

FLOUNCE SCARF

NORO SILK GARDEN

Materials
2 x 50g balls Noro Silk Garden (45% Silk, 45% Kid Mohair, 10% Lamb's Wool) (100m to 50g).
Needless: 5mm
Tension: 16sts to 10cm.
Abbreviation: Wrap—Slip next stitch on to right needle purlwise (put point of needle into front of stitch), yarn forward, return slipped stitch to left needle, yarn back.

Instructions
Scarf
- Using 5mm needles cast on 18 stitches.
- Row 1: Knit.
- Row 2: Purl.
- Row 3: Knit 15 stitches, wrap, turn.
- Row 4: Purl to end of row (15 stitches).
- Row 5: Knit 12 stitches, wrap, turn.
- Row 6: Purl to end of row (12 stitches).
- Row 7: Knit 9 stitches, wrap, turn.
- Row 8: Purl to end of row (9 stitches).
- Row 9: Knit 6 stitches, wrap, turn.
- Row 10: Purl to end of row (6 stitches).
- Row 11: Knit 3 stitches, wrap turn.
- Row 12: Purl to end of row (3 stitches).
- Row 13: Knit 1, *Knit 2, insert needle into the wrap as if to knit, then into the wrapped stitch, and knit both loops together, repeat from *4 times, knit to end.
- Row 14: Purl.
- Row 15: Knit across all 18 stitches.
- Row 16: Purl.
- Repeat rows 3 to 16 till work measures desired length, approximately 142cm.
- Cast off.
- Press with iron on wool setting.

INTERMEDIATE

FLOUNCE SCARF

WOOL BLEND

Photo: Wool Blend - grey

Materials

1 x 100g ball King Cole Riot double knitting (30% wool, 70% Premium Acrylic) (324 yards, 294 metres).
Needles: 4.5mm
Tension: 20sts to 10cm.
Abbreviation: Wrap—Slip next stitch on to right needle purlwise (put point of needle into front of stitch), yarn forward, return slipped stitch to left needle, yarn back.

Instructions

Scarf

- Using 4.5mm needles cast on 18 stitches.
- Row 1: Knit.
- Row 2: Purl.
- Row 3: Knit 15 stitches, wrap, turn.
- Row 4: Purl to end of row (15 stitches).
- Row 5: Knit 12 stitches, wrap, turn.
- Row 6: Purl to end of row (12 stitches).
- Row 7: Knit 9 stitches, wrap, turn.
- Row 8: Purl to end of row (9 stitches).
- Row 9: Knit 6 stitches, wrap, turn.
- Row 10: Purl to end of row (6 stitches).
- Row 11: Knit 3 stitches, wrap turn.
- Row 12: Purl to end of row (3 stitches).
- Row 13: Knit 1, *Knit 2, insert needle into the wrap as if to knit, then into the wrapped stitch, and knit both loops together, repeat from *4 times, knit to end.
- Row 14: Purl.
- Row 15: Knit across all 18 stitches.
- Row 16: Purl.
- Repeat rows 3 to 16 till work measures desired length, approximately 135cm for short multi-coloured version pictured on page 50 or 190cm for the long grey version of the scarf, which you can fold in half and loop the ends through, pictured on this page.
- Cast off.
- Press with iron on silk setting.

INTERMEDIATE

FLOUNCE SCARF

NORO KUREYON SOCK YARN

Photo: Flounce Scarf

Materials

2 x 100g ball Noro Silk Kureyon Sock Yarn (420m,100g, 70% wool, 30% nylon).

Needles: 3.75mm

Abbreviation: Wrap—Slip next stitch on to right needle purlwise (put point of needle into front of stitch), yarn forward, return slipped stitch to left needle, yarn back.

Instructions

Scarf

- Using 3.75mm needles cast on 20 stitches.
- Row 1: Knit.
- Row 2: Purl.
- Row 3: Knit 16 stitches, wrap, turn.
- Row 4: Purl to end of row (16 stitches).
- Row 5: Knit 12 stitches, wrap, turn.
- Row 6: Purl to end of row (12 stitches).
- Row 7: Knit 8 stitches, wrap, turn.
- Row 8: Purl to end of row (8 stitches).
- Row 9: Knit 4 stitches, wrap, turn.
- Row 10: Purl to end of row (4 stitches).
- Row 11: Knit 4 stitches, wrap turn.
- Row 12: Purl to end of row (4 stitches).
- Row 13; Knit 1, *Knit 2, insert needle into the wrap as if to knit, then into the wrapped stitch, and knit both loops together, repeat from *3 times, knit 4.
- Row 14: Purl.
- Row 15: Knit across all 20 stitches.
- Row 16: Purl.
- Repeat rows 3 to 16 till work measures desired length, approximately 158cm.
- Cast off.
- Press with iron on wool setting.

Photo: Ribbon Yarn Wrap

INTERMEDIATE

RIBBON YARN WRAP

Yarn: Ribbon Yarn Wrap

Materials

3 x 50g balls Online Linie Collection 103 Allegro (45% Schuwolle, 45% Polyamid, 10% Polyester) 70 metres per 50gm, Shade 0006.

Needles: 8mm

Instructions

- » Cast on 35 stitches.
- » Knit till work measures length from shoulder to shoulder when stretched.
- » Knit 2 together at end of next and following alternate rows till work measures length around shoulders when stretched.
- » Cast off.
- » For fringe: Cut 32cm lengths of yarn.
- » Attach fringe along lower edge.
- » Dimensions given are for item when not stretched.
- » Secure two ends together with a brooch over one shoulder.

Diagram

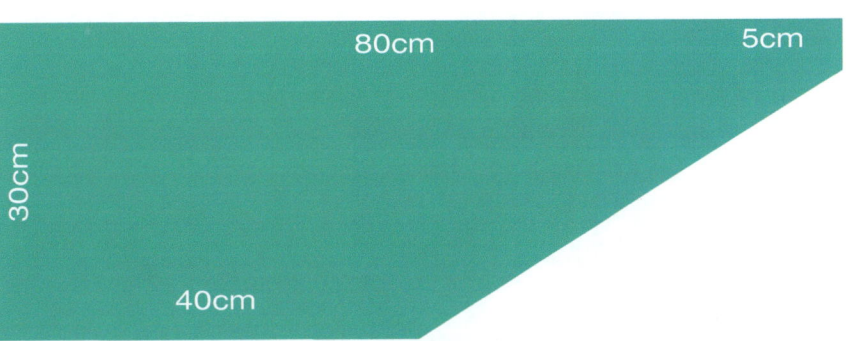

Photo: Bella

INTERMEDIATE

BELLA

Materials

- 1 X 100g hank Touch Exclusive Kid Mohair/Merino boucle (74% Kid Mohair/ 20%, Merino/ 6%, Binder) (175m per 100g), colour black.
- 1 x RichMore Excellent Mohair (Count 10) Graduation (76% mohair, 24% nylon) 2ply (199m per 20g).
- 1 x 50g ball Filatura Di Crosa Multicolor 60% Mohair 40% Acrylic (80m per 50g), weight DK.
- 1 x 50g ball Patons Mohair Mirage, 78% Mohair, 13% wool, 9% nylon (98m per 50g).
- 2 x 50g balls Moda Vera Tiramisu 77% Acrylic, 23% virgin wool (60m per 50g).
- 1 x 100g Hank Hawthorne Cottage Yarns Hand Spun Chunky Wool 100% wool, colour 7, (50m per 100g)

Needles: 6mm

Crochet hook: 6mm

Sizes: Small, Medium.

Measurements: Small 28cm x 100cm; Medium 30cm x 110cm.

Yarn: Bella

Instructions

- Using 6mm needles and Touch Kid Mohair/Merino cast on 107sts (117sts).
- Using Moda Vera Tiramisu knit one row.
- Using Multicolor knit one row.
- Using Patons Mohair Mirage knit one row.
- Using Touch Kid Mohair/Merino together with RichMore Excellent Mohair knit one row.
- Using second ball of Tiramisu knit one row.
- Using Hawthorne Cottage Chunky Wool (feature yarn)
- *knit 1, slip 1 repeat from *till last stitch, knit 1.
- Continue knitting single rows of each yarn randomly changing yarns (pick up yarn furthest from needle) but spacing feature yarn and black boucle evenly, till work measures 28cm (30cm).
- Cast off tightly.
- Using a 6mm crochet hook and Moda Vera Tiramisu work 1 row of double crochet along edges covering yarns carried along side of work.
- Attach top left corner to top right corner.

Photo: Multi Yarn Wrap 1

INTERMEDIATE

MULTI YARN WRAP

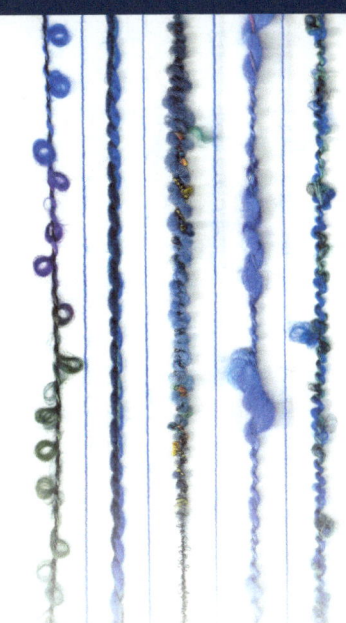

Multi Yarn Wrap 1

Materials

1 x 100g hank handspun or hand dyed multi-coloured slubby wool.

4 x 50g balls thick fancy yarns such as 12ply mohair, bulky acrylic/polyester or thick boucle.

5 x 25gm balls assorted thin yarns such as 2ply wool or fine mohair.

2ply wool in a great range of colours can be purchased from the Australian Tapestry Workshop (www.austapestry.com.au).

Needles: 12mm circular needle (80cm)

9mm circular needle (80cm)

Instructions

- Cast on 135 stitches using 12mm needle and thick fancy yarn.
- Carrying yarn not in use loosely along side of work. All rows can be started from either end of circular needle.
- Row 1: Knit using 9mm needle and thin yarn.
- Row 2: Knit using 12mm needle and a second thick fancy yarn.
- Row 3: Knit using 9mm needle and a second thin yarn (or slide stitches to other end of needle and use first thin yarn again).
- Row 4: Knit using 12mm needle and a third thick fancy yarn.
- Row 5: Knit using 9mm needle and a third thin yarn.
- Row 6: Knit using 12mm needle and Slubby yarn.
- Row 7: Knit using 9mm needle and a fourth thin yarn.
- Row 8: Knit using 12mm needle and fourth thick yarn.
- Row 9: Knit using 9mm needle and fifth thin yarn.
- Row 10: Knit using 12mm needle and the first thick fancy yarn used to cast on.
- Repeat rows 1-10, 5 times finishing by casting off loosely on row 10 of the fifth repeat.

- **Fringe**
- Cut 50cm lengths of 5 thick yarns.
- Attach fringe, alternating each of the 5 thick yarns, to ends of wrap (covering yarns carried along side edge of work).

Photo: Multi Yarn Wrap 2

Multi Yarn Wrap 2

Multi Yarn Wrap 3

Photo: Multi Yarn Wrap 3

Photo: Scarf & Hat in Shades of Autumn

INTERMEDIATE

SCARF & HAT IN SHADES OF AUTUMN

Yarn: Shades of Autumn

Materials

» 2 x 100g balls Patons Shadow Tweed 56% Wool, 40% Acrylic, 4% Viscose (133m per 100g) Colour 6906.

» 2 x 50g balls Moda Vera Diane 67% Acrylic, 14% Wool, 9% Mohair (150m per 50g) Colour: "Red Mix" Orange/ Mauve.

Needles: 9mm

Instructions

Scarf

» Cast on 14sts.
» Knit 1 row.
» Second and all following rows: *Knit 1, knit 1 into stitch below (insert right hand needle through the centre of the stitch below the next stitch to be knitted and knit, so that both stitches are knitted at the same time), repeat from *to last 2 stitches, knit 2.
» Continue till work measures 179cm.
» Cast off maintaining pattern in cast off row.

Hat

Brim

» Cast on 16 stitches.
» First row knit.
» Second and all following rows: *Knit 1, knit 1 into stitch below (insert right hand needle through the centre of the stitch below the next stitch to be knitted and knit, so that both stitches are knitted at the same time), repeat from *to last 2 stitches, knit 2.
» Continue till work measures length around head (56cm).
» Cast off maintaining pattern in cast off row.
» Sew cast on row to cast off row.

Crown of Hat

» Cast on 14 stitches.
» First row knit.
» Second and all following rows: *Knit 1, knit 1 into stitch below (insert right hand needle through the centre of the stitch below the next stitch to be knitted and knit, so that both stitches are knitted at the same time), repeat from *to last 2 stitches, knit 2.
» Continue till work measures 15cm.
» Cast off maintaining pattern in cast off row.
» Sew crown to brim of hat, easing into shape, rounding corners of crown as you sew.

Crown Diagram 15cm × 18cm

Brim Diagram 56cm × 22cm

Photo: Fuzzy Scarf & Hat

BEGINNERS

FUZZY SCARF & HAT

Yarn: Fuzzy Scarf & Hat

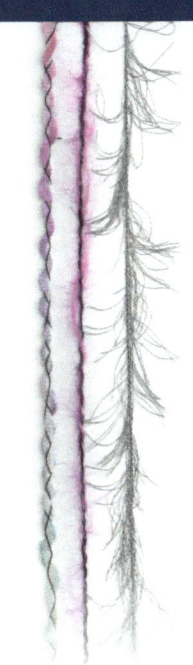

Materials

Scarf

- 3 x 50g balls 8ply multi-coloured acrylic yarn pink/peppermint/apricot.
- 2 x 50g balls 12ply Mohair in deep pink.
- 2 x 50g balls Patons Ostrich 100% Polyester, Colour Silver Grey.

Needles: 15mm

Instructions

- Cast on 16sts using all three yarns together.
- First row and following rows: *Knit 2, Purl 2, repeat from *till end of row.
- Continue till work measures 165cm.
- Cast off maintaining pattern in cast off row.

Hat

Brim

- Cast on 16sts using all three yarns together.
- First row and following rows: *Knit 2, Purl 2, repeat from *till end of row.
- Continue till work measures 56cm (or length around head).
- Cast off maintaining pattern in cast off row.

Crown

- Cast on 16sts using all three yarns together.
- First row and following rows: *Knit 2, Purl 2, repeat from *till end of row.
- Continue till work measures 16cm.
- Cast off maintaining pattern in cast off row.
- Sew two ends of brim piece together. Sew crown to brim.

Brim Diagram

56cm × 22cm

Crown Diagram

14cm × 16cm

Photo: Sunset Scarf

INTERMEDIATE

SUNSET SCARF

Yarn: Sunset Scarf

Materials

- 1 x 50g ball Naturally Colourworks 14ply 100% Pure Wool (50m per 50g) Shade 987.
- 2 x 50g balls Lincraft Winter Warmth 100% Acrylic Mohair (78m per 50g).

Needle: 6.5mm circular

Instructions

- Using Colourworks Wool cast on 200 stitches.
- Rows 1-4: Using Winter Warmth knit 4 rows.
- Row 5: Using Colourworks Wool knit 1 row.
- Rows 6-10: Using second ball of Winter Warmth repeat rows 1-5.
- Continue repeating these 10 rows 8 times.
- Using Winter Warmth knit 3 rows and cast off loosely.

Photo: Moth Cocoon

BEGINNERS

MOTH COCOON

Yarn: Moth Cocoon

Materials

- 2 x 50g balls Moda Vera Riccio 30% Wool, 55% acrylic, 15% polyamide (65m per 50g).
- 2 x 50g balls Lincraft Romania yarn 85% acrylic, 15% polyester (65m per 50g).

Needles: 9mm

Instructions

- Using Romania cast on 95sts.
- Knit 1 row.
- Using Riccio knit 2 rows.
- Using Romania knit 2 rows.
- Repeat last 4 rows till work measures 25cm.
- Cast off.
- Piece measures approximately 132cm x 25cm.
- Sew right-hand side edge (C-D) to beginning of cast off row (A-B) as shown in diagram.

Diagram

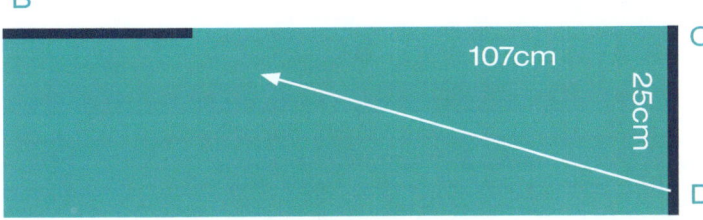

Photo: Butterfly Cocoon

INTERMEDIATE

BUTTERFLY COCOON

Yarn: Butterfly Cocoon

Materials

Main Colour

The first two yarns used together form the main colour.

1 x 100g ball Marta's Yarns Bubble (78% Kid Mohair, 13% Wool, 9% Nylon) 100 metres per 50gm. Blue/green.

2 x 50g balls Adriafil Graphic (75% wool, 15% acrylic, 10% polyamide) 70m per 50gm. Colour Blue Multi.

Contrast colour: 2 x 100g hanks Marta's Yarns Slubby multi-colour blue/green.

Needles: 20mm

Instructions

» Cast on 18sts, using main colour (Bubble and Graphic yarns together).

» Knit 4 rows.

» Using contrast yarn (Slubby) knit 2 rows.

» Repeat these 6 rows till work measures length around shoulders.

» Cast off.

» Sew cast off row (A-B) to beginning of side edge (C-D) as shown in diagram.

Diagram

The peak can be worn at the front or back.

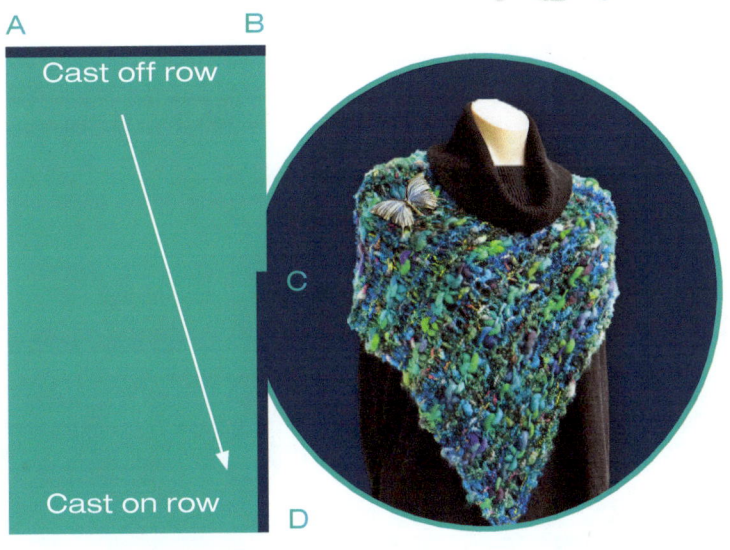

© Copyright 2016 Susan Johnson — Creative Knitting for all Seasons and Yarns

Photo: Dragonfly Wrap

BEGINNERS

DRAGONFLY WRAP

Yarn: Dragonfly Wrap

Materials

- 4 x 50g balls Patons Loopy (83% Mohair, 17% Acrylic) 40m per 50g.
- 3 x 50g Lincraft Venice (11% Polyamide, 89% Acrylic) 65m per 50g.

Needles: 8mm

Measurements: 44cm x 140cm.

Instructions

- Using 8mm needles and Venice yarn cast on 45sts.
- Knit 1 row.
- Using Loopy knit 2 rows.
- Using Venice yarn knit 2 rows.
- Repeat last 4 rows till work measures 140cm.
- Cast off.

Photo: Bobbly Wrap

BEGINNERS

BOBBLY WRAP

Yarn: Bobbly Wrap

Materials

- 5 x 50g balls Moda Vera Jacki (55% acrylic, 45% wool) (37m per 50g) (thick yarn).
- 1 x 50g ball multi-coloured lightweight mohair boucle (thin yarn).

Needles: 12mm circular and 6.5mm circular

Tension: 8sts to 10cm.

Instructions

Wrap

- Using thick yarn (Moda Vera Jacki) and thick needle (12mm circular needle) cast on 32sts.
- Row 1: Using thin needle (6.5 mm circular needle) and thin yarn (lightweight mohair boucle) knit one row.
- *Row 2: Slide stitches to other end of circular needle and begin this row using thick yarn and thick needle, knit row.
- Row 3: Slide stitches to other end of needle and begin this row using thin yarn and thin needle knit row.
- Repeat from *till work measures approximately 114cm.
- Cast off using thick yarn and thick needle.

Photo: Pastel Scarf

INTERMEDIATE

PASTEL SCARF

Materials

- 1 x 100g hank multi-coloured 12ply Mohair pale blue/ mauve/pink.
- 2 x 50g balls 2ply Wool.

Needles: 20mm

Instructions

- Cast on 10sts using mohair and 2 strands of wool together.
- Pattern: (Begins with multiple of 2 stitches).
- Row 1: knit.
- Second and all following rows: *Knit 1, knit 1 into stitch below (insert right hand needle through the centre of the stitch below the next stitch to be knitted and knit, so that both stitches are knitted at the same time), repeat from *to last 2 stitches, knit 2.
- Continue till work measures 165cm or length desired.
- Cast off maintaining pattern in cast off row.

Photo: Butterfly Blanket & Framed Butterflies

ADVANCED

BUTTERFLY BLANKET

Yarn: Butterfly Blanket

Materials

- » 6 x 50g balls 8ply/DK Wool (120m/50g) Main Colour (MC) (Yarn featured is Marta's Yarns Metro Wool 8ply/DK Rainbow fuschia pink colour 109).

- » 6 x 50g balls 8ply/DK Wool (120m/50g) Contrast Colour 1 (CC1) (Yarn featured is Marta's Yarns Metro Wool 8ply/DK Rainbow lime green colour 124).

- » 6 x 50g balls 8ply/DK Wool (120m/50g) Contrast Colour 2 (CC2) (Yarn featured is Marta's Yarns Metro 8ply/DK Rainbow royal blue colour 115).

Materials for Shaded Butterflies

- » 1 x 50g ball 8ply/DK Wool (120m/50g) of each of 1st, 2nd, 3rd and 4th graduated shades of green (shades 119, 120, 121, 122) (emerald, spring, leaf, lime) (4 balls in total).

- » 1 x 50g ball 8ply/DK Wool (120m/50g) of each of 1st, 2nd, 3rd and 4th graduated shades of purple (shades 111, 112, 113, 114) (red purple, mid purple, purple, blue purple) (4 balls in total).

- » 1 x 50g ball 8ply/DK Wool (120m/50g) of each of 1st, 2nd, 3rd and 4th graduated shades of orange (shades 106, 105, 104, 103) (brick, orange, pumpkin, yellow) (4 balls in total).

Butterfly Square 1 (B1)

- » Fuschia pink background and 4 shades of green butterfly (1st and 21st squares on chart).

- » Knit in colourway 1 as follows:

- » Background Colour (BC) fuschia pink (Yarn featured is Marta's Yarns Metro 8ply/DK Rainbow colour 109).

© Copyright 2016 Susan Johnson

Butterfly Blanket (Cont'd)

- Four graduated shades of green as follows:
- Shade 1: (SH1) (Yarn featured is Marta's Yarns Metro 8ply/DK Rainbow colour 119) (emerald).
- Shade 2: (SH2) (Yarn featured is Marta's Yarns Metro 8ply/DK Rainbow colour 120) (spring).
- Shade 3: (SH3) (Yarn featured is Marta's Yarns Metro 8ply/DK Rainbow colour 121) (leaf).
- Shade 4: (SH4) (Yarn featured is Marta's Yarns Metro 8ply/DK Rainbow colour 122) (mid lime).

Butterfly Square 2 (B2)

- Lime green background and 4 shades of purple butterfly (6th and 23rd squares on chart).
- Knit in colourway 2 as follows:
- Background Colour (BC) colour 124 lime green.
- Four shades of purple as follows:
- Shade 1: (SH1) (Yarn featured is Marta's Yarns Metro 8ply/DK Rainbow colour 111) (red purple).
- Shade 2: (SH2) (Yarn featured is Marta's Yarns Metro 8ply/DK Rainbow colour 112) (mid purple).
- Shade 3: (SH3) (Yarn featured is Marta's Yarns Metro 8ply/DK Rainbow colour 113) (purple).
- Shade 4: (SH4) (Yarn featured is Marta's Yarns Metro 8ply/DK Rainbow colour 114) (blue purple).

Butterfly Square 3 (B3)

- Royal blue background and 4 shades of orange butterfly (11th and 33rd squares on chart).
- Knit in colourway 3 as follows:
- Background Colour (BC) colour 115 royal blue.
- Four shades of orange as follow:
- Shade 1: (SH1) (Yarn featured is Marta's Yarns Metro 8ply/DK Rainbow colour 106) (brick).
- Shade 2: (SH2) (Yarn featured is Marta's Yarns Metro 8ply/DK Rainbow colour 105) (orange).
- Shade 3: (SH3) (Yarn featured is Marta's Yarns Metro 8ply/DK Rainbow colour 104) (pumpkin).
- Shade 4: (SH4) (Yarn featured is Marta's Yarns Metro 8ply/DK Rainbow colour 103) (yellow).
- **Needles:** 6mm and 4mm or size to obtain gauge.
- **Tension:** 15 stitches and 20 rows to 10cm.

Instructions

Starting from left bottom edge of chart work blanket in vertical strips, following colour chart, as follows:

Strip 1

Squares 1-7 shown in blanket diagram.

Square 1

- Using 6mm needles and two strands together of Main Colour (MC) fuschia pink, cast on 27 stitches.
- Butterfly Square 1 (B1) fuschia pink background with shaded green butterfly square.
- Row 1: *Knit 1, Purl 1, repeat from *till end of row, knit 1.
- Rows 2-6: Repeat row 1.
- Row 7: Knit 1, purl 1, knit 1, purl 1, knit 19 stitches, purl 1, knit 1, purl 1, knit 1.
- Row 8: Knit 1, purl 1, knit 1, purl 1, purl 19 stitches, purl 1, knit 1, purl 1, knit 1.
- Commence butterfly.

Butterfly Blanket Diagram

7	14	B1	28	35
B2	13	20	27	34
5	12	19	26	B3
4	B3	18	25	32
3	10	17	24	31
2	9	16	B2	30
B1	8	15	22	29

Butterfly Blanket (Cont'd)

- » Rows 9-30: Knit 1, purl 1, knit 1, purl 1. Work next 19 stitches from chart for butterfly, in Colourway 1 (fuschia pink background and butterfly in shades of green), purl 1, knit 1, purl 1, knit 1.
- » Rows 33-34: repeat rows 7 and 8.
- » Rows 33-38: Repeat row 1 six times.

Square 2
Plain blue square

- » Change to CC2 (blue) using two strands together.
- » Row 1: *Knit 1, Purl 1, repeat from *till end of row, knit 1.
- » Rows 2-6: Repeat row 1.
- » Row 7: Knit 1, purl 1, knit 1, purl 1, knit 19 stitches, purl 1, knit 1, purl 1, knit 1.
- » Row 8: Knit 1, purl 1, knit 1, purl 1, purl 19 stitches, purl 1, knit 1, purl 1, knit 1.
- » Repeat rows 7 and 8 twelve times.
- » Rows 33-38: Repeat row 1 six times.

Square 3
Lime green square

- » Change to CC1 (lime green) using two strands together.
- » Repeat square 2.

Square 4
Plain Fuschia Pink Square

- » Change to MC (fuschia pink) using two strands together.
- » Repeat square 2.

Square 5
Plain Royal Blue Square

- » Change to CC2 (royal blue) using two strands together.
- » Repeat square 2.

Square 6
Butterfly Square 2 (B2)

- » Change to CC1 (lime green), for background colour, using two strands together.
- » Repeat square 1 using 4 shades of purple for butterfly.

Square 7
Plain Fuschia Pink Square

- » Change to MC (fuschia pink) using two strands together.
- » Repeat square 2.
- » Cast off.

Strip 2

- » Squares 8-14: form strip 2.
- » Squares are knitted with the colours in the following sequence:
- » Square 8: Plain CC2 royal blue.
- » Square 9: Plain CC1 lime green.
- » Square 10: Plain MC fuschia pink.
- » Square 11: Butterfly Square 3 (B3) royal blue background with 4 shades of orange butterfly.
- » Square 12: Plain CC1 lime green.
- » Square 13: Plain MC fuschia pink.
- » Square 14: Plain CC2 royal blue.

Strips 3-5

- » Following diagram complete strips 3 to 5 placing shaded butterflies (one in each strip) as charted.

6 Backing Squares for 6 Butterfly Squares

- » Using Background Colour of each of the Butterfly Squares make 6 Backing Squares as follows:

Butterfly Blanket (Cont'd)

- Using 4mm needles cast on 21 stitches.
- Row 1: Knit.
- Row 2: Knit 1, purl to last stitch, knit 1.
- Continue in stocking stitch, repeating rows 1 and 2, with one knit stitch at beginning and end of each row, till work measures height of completed butterfly square.

Sew 6 backing squares to centre of 6 butterfly squares, attaching at inner edge of moss stitch border, covering back of intarsia butterfly.

Sew 5 strips together.

Butterfly Blanket Chart

Key: Shade 1 (purple), Shade 2 (green), Shade 3 (blue), Shade 4 (orange). NB: Each grid square = 1 stitch of 2 strands of yarn.

Photo: Framed butterflies

ADVANCED

FRAMED BUTTERFLIES

Instructions

- » Using 6mm needles and 2 strands of main colour of butterfly square to be knitted cast on 27 stitches.
- » Knit as for Butterfly Squares 1, 2 and 3 for blanket.
- » Cast off.
- » Press with iron on wool setting.
- » Frame.

INTERMEDIATE

BUTTERFLY CUSHION

Photo: Butterfly Cushion

Materials

- 10 x 50g balls 8ply Cleakheaton Country Pure New wool (95m/50g).

Needles: 7mm

Tension: 12.5sts to 10cm.

Measurements: Cushion cover measures 52cm x 52cm (fits 20inch/50cm cushion insert).

Knitting Stitches:

Stocking stitch:

- Row 1: On right side knit.
- Row 2: On wrong side purl.
- Repeat these 2 rows.

Reverse stocking stitch:

- Row 1: On right side Purl.
- Row 2: On wrong side Knit.
- Repeat these 2 rows.

Moss stitch:

- Row 1: *k1p1, repeat from *to end of row.
- Row 2: **p1, k1, repeat from **to end of row.
- Repeat these 2 rows.

Instructions

- Using 2 strands of wool together cast on 64 stitches.
- Work 8 rows moss stitch.
- Work 58 rows reverse stocking stitch.
- Next row purl 8 stitches for reverse stocking stitch border, knit 48 stitches (stocking stitch), purl 8 stitches for reverse stocking stitch border.
- Maintaining 8 stitches reverse stocking stitch border at each edge work 11 more rows.
- Next row purl 8 stitches for reverse stocking stitch border, knit 5 stitches, starting with the next stitch (i.e. the 14th stitch of the row) begin row 1 of butterfly from chart working from right to left of chart on right side and left to right of chart on wrong side (x indicates purl stitch on right side and knit stitch on wrong side) till last 13 stitches, knit 5 stitches, purl 8 stitches for reverse stocking stitch border.
- Maintaining 8 stitch reverse stocking stitch border work remaining 59 rows of butterfly pattern.
- *Next row work 8 stitches reverse stocking stitch border, work 48 stitches stocking stitch, work 8 stitches reverse stocking stitch border.
- Repeat from *11 times.
- Knit 58 rows reverse stocking stitch.
- Work 4 rows moss stitch.
- Next row make buttonholes.
- Buttonhole row: Keeping moss stitch pattern correct ** work 9sts, knit 2 together, yarn around needle, repeat from **6 times work to end of row.
- Work 3 rows moss stitch.
- Cast off.
- Fold cast off edge to meet finish of first moss stitch border (8 rows from cast on edge).
- Sew side seams overlapping moss stitch borders at centre back of cushion.
- Sew on 6 buttons.

Butterfly Cushion Chart

Photo: Flounce Scarf (Wool Blend)
Instructions on page 14

CONTRIBUTORS

Natalie Davies *(Photographer)*

Natalie Davies is a highly successful wedding and portrait photographer. Natalie completed a Diploma of Arts in Applied Photography and has experience in several leading Melbourne studios providing the foundation for a technically proficient and professional result. Natalie established her own business over ten years ago on the Mornington Peninsula in Melbourne.

Visit www.nataliedaviesphotography.com to learn more about Natalie and view her beautiful work.

David Smyth *(Photographer)*

(Butterfly images and photos of designs on mannequins)

David Smyth is a freelance photographer based in Melbourne. After completing a bachelor degree in Visual Communication there was a natural gravitation towards photography. 'Photography is a very accessible medium to capture a generalised representation of things that are incomprehensible in time and space'

See David's work at
www.flickr.com/photos/dbsmyth

Michelle Johnson *(Model)*

Michelle Johnson has studied Studio Arts, Photography, Dance and completed a Diploma of Children's Services. Modelling is just one of Michelle's many talents. She has danced professionally Salsa and Latin style dances. Michelle draws and photographs children's portraits and utilizes her creative talents in her work caring for babies and young children.

Nelly Murariu *(Graphic Designer)*

Nelly Murariu is a graphic designer specialising in book cover design and book formatting. After experiencing different jobs, including working on cruise ships for a few years, she has found her true calling: freelance graphic design. She is the founder of PixBeeDesign.com and she works with people from all over the world to create beautiful eye catching designs.

Visit Nelly's website at
www.PixBeeDesign.com

Jodie Zidar *(Graphic Designer)*

Jodie Zidar, a graphic designer and website developer, is the creative mind behind Jaz Effect Design. Jodie started her career as a Personal Assistant before moving into Public Relations where she worked on many diverse projects in the field of multi-media production, photography, and Graphic Design. After completing a Diploma in Graphic Design, she established Jaz Effect Design.

To view more of Jodie's work,
visit www.jazeffect.com.au

www.ingramcontent.com/pod-product-compliance
Lightning Source LLC
Chambersburg PA
CBHW041627170426
43195CB00034B/83